Understanding
Boat Diesel
Engines

Understanding Boat Diesel Engines

JOHN C. PAYNE

SHERIDAN HOUSE

This edition first published 2005 by
Sheridan House Inc.
145 Palisade Street,
Dobbs Ferry, NY 10522
www.sheridanhouse.com

Library of Congress Cataloging-In-Publication Data

Payne, John C.
    Understanding boat diesel engines / John C. Payne.
        p. cm.
    ISBN 1-57409-200-6 (alk. paper)
        1. Marine diesel motors—Maintenance and repair—Handbooks,
    manuals, etc. 2. Boats and boating—Electrical equipment—
    Handbooks, manuals, etc. I. Title.
    VM771.P38 2005
    623.87'236'0288—dc22   2004021016

Printed in the United States of America
ISBN 1-57409-200-6

CONTENTS

1. BASIC DIESEL THEORY

The diesel was invented back in 1892, and named after the pioneering German engineer, Rudolph Diesel. He demonstrated the engine using peanut oil at the World's Fair in 1900. The diesel engine works on the principle of compression-ignition. Air is compressed to a point where fuel combustion will occur spontaneously. This book covers 4-stroke compression-ignition engines.

What does 4-stroke mean?

A diesel engine has four distinct phases to each cycle. The 4-stroke cycle comprises the air intake or as it is sometimes called, the induction stroke; the compression stroke; the power stroke; and the exhaust stroke.

The air intake (induction) stroke

In the induction stroke, the piston moves down and the air is sucked into the cylinder. At Top Dead Center (TDC), the inlet valves open and the air required for fuel combustion is drawn in through the air inlet manifold, air filter and turbocharger as the piston moves downwards. At the bottom of the stroke, Bottom Dead Center (BDC), the inlet valves close, sealing the cylinder full of fresh air.

The compression stroke

In the compression stroke, the piston moves upwards to compress the air. This raises the air temperature within the engine cylinder, typically to around 1025°F (550°C). Fuel injection takes place just before TDC and ceases after an interval.

The power stroke

The fuel is injected into the heated and compressed air within the cylinder as a stream of small droplets. It ignites spontaneously when the droplets mix with the heated air. Once ignited, combustion occurs and increased pressure is generated in the cylinder. This drives explosively the piston downward to BDC. This produces the power to turn the crankshaft and therefore the shaft and propeller.

The exhaust stroke

At BDC, the exhaust valves open to expel exhaust gases. The piston travels back up, forcing the exhaust gases out through the valves into the exhaust system. At the end of the upward stroke, the valves close at TDC. This process is sometimes called gas exchange. The exhaust valves are controlled by pushrods and a camshaft and the crankshaft, at every second engine revolution. The camshaft rotates at half the speed of the crankshaft.

2. THE FUEL SYSTEM

Engine combustion is significantly influenced by the design of the fuel injection system. The fuel is drawn from the fuel tank, through pre-filters or separators and the engine fuel filter to the fuel pumps. The pressurized fuel is then fed to the injectors. Although fuel is injected as a liquid, the correct vaporization is necessary for efficiency. This requires thorough and rapid mixing of both the hot compressed air and the fuel vapor. Injection pressures will be in the range of 2500 to 7000 lbs psi. On some engines excess fuel is then fed back or returned to the fuel tank.

Figure 1-1 Fuel System Installation
Courtesy of Vetus

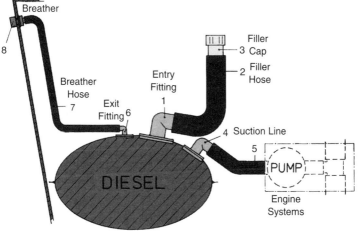

What are the fuel system components?

The typical boat fuel system comprises several main components.

1. **Fuel Oil Tank.** This is the main tank or tanks where you load the fuel through the deck filler. The deck filler cap must seal well and must be watertight. The tank should have a vent or breather to prevent pressure or partial vacuum formation. This must be located above the waterline to prevent water ingress. The tank should be angled so that water and sediment can collect and can be drained off with a drain cock. These should be checked at least monthly. Tanks should be kept as full as possible at all times to reduce condensation. In addition, a full tank reduces the amount of fuel movement or slopping that can cause aeration, or can stir up debris trapped within a tank.

2. **Header or Day Tank.** Some boats have a tank where fuel is transferred from the main tank. This tank is often mounted higher than the engine to allow a positive gravity feed to the engine.

3. **The fuel pre-filter/separator.** This is installed before fuel enters the engine. The Racor and Dahl filters are commonly used. They trap oil, water and debris before they even reach the engine filters. These are easily drained through a plug.

About the engine fuel system

1. **The Fuel Lift Pump.** Its main role is to ensure adequate fuel supplies for combustion. This pump is also used to bleed the engine with its manual operating lever.

2. **The Engine Fuel Filter.** This is a fine filter mounted on the engine. It is essential to keep the fuel element clean. This is the most important step in maintaining fuel oil quality. Always fill the filter with fuel, if possible, and smear some fuel oil on the rubber sealing wing when renewing the disposable element.

3. **The Fuel Injection Pump.** This pump pressurizes the fuel to the injectors. It also meters the correct fuel quantity at the precise time it is required at the top of the compression stroke. The pump is a precision piece of equipment. Both dirt and water will seriously damage the pump.

4. **The Injectors.** These inject atomized fuel oil into the cylinder. The injector is a precision piece of equipment. It will spray the fine fuel mist into the cylinder in a designated spray pattern to properly distribute fuel for optimum combustion efficiency.

What about fuel injection?

The quantity of fuel delivered at each injection is controlled by the injection pressure, the injector nozzle orifice area, and the time at which the nozzle valve lifts. To increase the vaporization rate, the fuel must be injected into the cylinder as an atomized stream of fuel droplets. The fuel injector must also meter the correct quantity of fuel to match the engine power requirements, and the injection period must be determined precisely. The droplet size of the fuel is critical to achieving good combustion. Large fuel droplets will require a longer period to vaporize delaying combustion. Small fuel droplets move relatively slowly, reducing the oxygen mixing times. Both conditions will lead to incomplete combustion, with reduced efficiency, increased noise and increased emissions.

How is an injector constructed?

The injector consists of several components that include the tappet, plunger, barrel, body, nozzle assembly (spring, check and tip), and the cartridge valve (solenoid, armature, poppet valve, and poppet spring). In mechanical systems, push rods and cam lobes activate rocker arms and the injector plunger and barrel. In electronic systems the ECM energizes the solenoid, which magnetically attracts the armature, lifts the poppet valve and allows fuel pressure to build up. The check lifts and is then injected via the nozzle assembly into the cylinder. At the programmed end of injection the solenoid valve de-energizes and fuel flow ceases.

What is a constant pressure injection system?

In the common rail injection system, the fuel is maintained at a constant pressure in the manifold. The manifold is connected to cam-actuated nozzles or a distributor, and a timing valve and pressure-activated injector nozzles. The pressure is maintained by compressing the diesel fuel, using a pump, and supplying fuel after each injection. The fuel is supplied from an accumulator and pressure-regulating valve, which may be governor controlled, or manually controlled.

What is an accumulator injection system?

The accumulator system uses both upper and lower plungers in a common bore. The lower plunger is driven by an eccentric cam and the upper plunger is spring-loaded. As the bottom plunger is forced up the fuel between the plungers is pressurized by the spring force applied to the top spring. Fuel will continue to pressurize until a delivery groove in the lower plunger indexes with the outlet passage. The pressurized fuel is then injected and continues until the upper spring forces the plunger downward and closes the outlet passage.

What is the jerk pump injection system?

The jerk pump injection system is the most common system in use for fuel pressurization, metering and timing. A camshaft activates the plungers and controls injection. The jerk pump system is the basis for distributor pumps and unit injectors. Engine makers such as Caterpillar use HEUI (Hydraulically Actuated, Electronically controlled, Unit Injector) which have fuel injection pressures in the range of 18-24,000 psi.

About indirect injection (IDI)

In the IDI engine, the air is drawn in through a specially shaped inlet port or prechamber connected to the cylinder top housing the fuel injector. This causes the air to swirl during compression and combustion starts. This slows the combustion rate and produces less noise The IDI engine has a greater fuel economy and turbocharging can enhance this. Useful speed range increases with larger valves, and noise is reduced.

About direct injection (DI)

The fuel is directly injected into the cylinder. The piston incorporates a toroidal depression, which is where combustion occurs. These engine types are the most efficient, and can deliver high power over small time periods; they are, however, noisier. They have relatively small acceleration, as both the inlet and exhaust valves are restricted in diameter to allow for a centrally located injector, and this inhibits the aspiration process. It also results in better economy and lower exhaust emissions.

How important is fuel quality?

The quality of the diesel fuel is critical to good engine combustion and the US standard for diesel is the American Society of Testing and Materials ASTM D 975. In practice the deterioration of fuel is almost inevitable, as contaminants will be introduced into the fuel system through mixing, transferring and storage. During transportation and storage, fuel is in contact with air and water vapor. Diesel fuel can undergo change as a result. This sometimes creates sludge, which may block the fuel filters, or form gums that can damage the fuel injection equipment or leave deposits within the engine. Low quality fuels also cause injector fouling. Simple hole injectors in a DI engine, when fouled, can change the spray patterns as the needles and seats become sticky, causing leakage, poor combustion and excess smoke. The pintle injectors within an IDI engine can also become fouled. If the needles and injector bodies are dirty, the initial small fuel burst does not occur and all the fuel is delivered at once.

Fuel contaminants

No.2-D diesel fuel is unfortunately one of variable quality and purity, ranging from very good to extremely poor. No.1-D is sometimes blended to improve cold temperature performance. The API specifications allow for acceptable levels of impurities such as sulfur, wax and other contaminants that include water, dirt and ash. Fuel contaminants are classified as either precipitates or particulates. The precipitates are commonly non-combustible materials that form when fuel oxidizes and since they are heavier than fuel, they normally fall to the bottom of fuel tanks. Particulates are also known as asphaltines, which are black tar-like substances that plug fuel filters. Wax is added to fuels; however in colder conditions this may thicken, and can gel causing fuel blockages.

What does ignition delay mean?

The normal method for describing ignition delay of a fuel is by the cetane number (CN). The longer the ignition delay, the lower the cetane number of the fuel. Fuel supplies are generally within the 45-55 CN range. The ignition delay period is crucial to engine starting. It can cause white smoke after start up, diesel knock at idle speeds and lowering overall engine performance.

About lubricity

The most important factor, assuming that the fuel is clean, is the viscosity. Very high fuel viscosities impose severe strains on the fuel system, in particular the fuel pump and injectors. Low viscosities will cause leakage past the fuel pump, as well as unnecessary wear of vital components, since fuel also acts as a lubricant. This factor is known as lubricity. Viscosity will impact on fuel combustion after injection, as this will also affect the fuel droplet size and spray pattern. Water is the worst and most common contaminant in fuel, destroying the lubrication qualities of the fuel and damaging fuel pumps and injectors.

How does sulfur affect the fuel quality?

The sulfur content is crucial in controlling exhaust emissions. In the combustion process, the sulfur compounds alter and mix with water to form acidic by-products, notably sulfur dioxide ($SO2$) and sulfur trioxide ($SO3$), which also enter the exhaust gas, causing pollution. High sulfur levels are corrosive and will cause high engine wear rates, and degrade the engine oil additives. High sulfur diesel has inadequate lubrication qualities and will reduce fuel injection component performance. Sulfur levels should not exceed 0.5% and should be less than .05%. If above 0.5%, maintenance intervals will have to be reduced for oil and filter changes.

How serious is water in the fuel?

The answer is a simple, very serious! Water in the fuel is the most common killer of diesel engines. Fuel tanks should always be topped up to reduce condensation, and where possible, tanks with a drain valve should have water drained off. After filling tanks, the pre-filters should be monitored for excess water, and drained. Bad fuel is a common occurrence. The most common method of water removal is stripping, which uses a silicon treated medium to inhibit water flow. The coalescing filter uses gravity to take water droplets out of the fuel. The absorption filters use a filter medium to absorb water out of the fuel. The more commonly installed filter/separators use the stripping method. You invest in reliability when you install a filter/separator, either a Parker Racor unit or a Baldwin Dahl unit.

How does the Dahl filter work?

1. Fuel from the tank enters the filter inlet port, and is directed down through the center tube. The depressurizer cone then spreads the fuel.

2. As fuel is discharged from the depressurizer cone, 80% of the contaminants are separated from the fuel. The fuel rises upward and most of the solid contaminants and water settle into the bowl's quiet zone. The system includes a reverse flow valve, to hold prime in the fuel system by not allowing flow back to the tank during shutdown. There is a removable primer plug at the top for use when complete priming is required.

3. As the fuel rises upward, remaining minute water droplets collect on the cone, baffle and bowl surfaces. The size and weight of the water droplets gradually increase causing downward flow into the sump.

4. Fuel is then filtered completely by the 2-micron paper element. The clean fuel continues up through the outlet port to the pump and injection system. The transparent bowl holds up to 24 ounces of water to reduce draining intervals, via the draincock.

How does the Racor filter work?

Racor filters work in three stages:

1. In the separation stage, a turbine separates large solids and free water using centrifugal force.

2. In the coalescing stage, the smaller water droplets and solids coalesce on a conical baffle and drop into the collection bowl.

3. The filtration stage uses a fine micron Aquabloc water-repelling paper element.

The units also have optional heaters and electrical water continuity probe alarm units, and a vacuum gauge to monitor pressure drop across filter elements.

Using fuel additives

The chemical makeup of fuel will determine the performance characteristics. There is no perfect fuel; it is a compromise. Additives are added to diesel to improve the ignition delay periods, giving improved combustion efficiency, less noise and smoke emissions. Detergents are added to keep the injectors clean and allow correct fuel metering. Anti-corrosive additives are used to protect the injection system, and anti-foam compounds are used to limit frothing. Uncontaminated fuel is essential to good combustion and efficient operation of the engine. There are many accounts of water-contaminated fuels being supplied to unsuspecting boats from bunker barges and fuel suppliers.

About microbe growth

Moisture and water within the system can encourage microbiotic growth within the fuel. Algae, fungi and bacteria, both aerobic and anaerobic, will multiply rapidly and plug the filters. Once the system is infected, considerable flushing is required if it is to be eliminated. The solution is to add chemical biocides to kill or maintain quality. There are devices on the market called magnetic biocides, such as the De-Bug. The theory is that single-celled organisms have electrical potential, usually positive on the cell wall and a negative interior. If this is disrupted the cell will die or rupture. This can be initiated by passing fuel over a strong permanent magnet or series of magnets. In the De-bug unit, the cells are exposed to 24 magnetic field changes within 20.2" of travel. The fluctuations destroy the cell by disruption of the cell ion and pH balances.

About fuel system bleeding

When any part of the fuel system is disconnected during maintenance or troubleshooting, and air has entered, all air must be bled from the system. Air within the fuel system can cause many problems and be difficult to expel. Air in the system will absorb the pump force and the injector will not open. The injector pump and injector operate by having hydraulic pressure applied that is high enough to open the needle valves. This allows fuel to enter under sufficient pressure to atomize for combustion. No attempt to start the engine should be made until the injection pump is properly filled and primed; damage can occur, as fuel acts as a lubricant for the fuel pump.

Some handy hints on bleeding

Paint the bleed screws with bright yellow paint to improve visibility in low light. Always have the correct or even dedicated spanners ready by the engine for use. Use caution with high-pressure fluids such as fuel; escaping pressurized fuel can penetrate the skin and cause serious injury leading to gangrene. When fuel oil is injected into the skin it must be surgically removed within hours. Tighten all connections before pressurizing the system.

The engine bleeding sequence

1. Check that the fuel tank has enough fuel.

2. Make sure all fuel system pipes and connections are tight.

3. Check all hoses, fuel line fittings and steel lines for damage as they may chafe during engine operation.

3. Loosen the bleed screw located on top of the engine fuel pre-filter or separator if one is installed.

4. Manually operate the thumb or hand-priming lever located on the lift pump until a steady stream of fuel flows. This should run bubble-free; initially there will be a lot of bubbles.

5. When finished, tighten the bleed screw.

6. Loosen the bleed screw on top of engine fuel filter. This is located after the fuel lift pump.

7. Manually operate the thumb or hand-priming lever located on the lift pump until a steady stream of fuel flows. This should run bubble-free; initially there will be a lot of bubbles.

8. When finished, tighten the bleed screw.

9. Repeat the bleeding process at the fuel injection pump inlet connection.

10. Loosen the bleed screws on the injection pump housing. This should be around 2-3 turns. Manually operate the lift pump until fuel is flowing without any bubbles.

11. Each injector must be bled and tightened in sequence. Start with the injector located at the end of the system from the inlet first. Tighten each in turn. Repeat this for each of the other injectors. Crack open the connections to allow air to bleed out.

12. Start the engine, and if it runs the remaining injectors should bleed automatically.

What is the injection delay period?

An important factor in combustion efficiency is the delay period between the fuel injection and the ignition. It is dependent on fuel quality, compression temperature, compression pressure, and the fuel droplet sizes. Injection delay is the time taken for the injection pump to build up pressure exceeding the opening pressure of the injector. It must be as short as possible. Both engine design and fuel quality are crucial, as they affect engine performance, cold start characteristics, warm-up times, engine power output, engine noise, and the level of exhaust emissions. Short ignition delays do not generally cause problems. Long delays will allow fuel to accumulate in the cylinder prior to ignition. When this occurs, the cylinder pressure will rise rapidly with incomplete and inefficient combustion. When delay is excessive, pressure rise is also fast, causing "knocking." During the final part of the combustion process the final fuel is burnt and temperatures and pressure are so high that the fuel droplets ignite at once. Good combustion efficiency ceases at this point.

How efficient is the engine?

Combustion efficiency is a measure of compression ratio, and is dependent on the control of ignition and fuel combustion. Factors controlling combustion are the air quantity, the fuel-air mixture, the compression temperature and the compression pressure. Efficiency and losses in the process relate to fuel energy, incomplete combustion, and air/fuel mixing of less than 100%, so that unburnt fuel will exit in the exhaust gases. Losses are typically around 65% and are higher at low loads than full-load operation. Sources of loss include leakage through piston rings, friction losses, heat losses through combustion chamber walls, incomplete expansion, thermal losses via exhaust gasses and incomplete combustion. The air temperature, the air humidity and the air pressure affect the power ratings of an engine. In many engine spaces, engine power is reduced due to lack of air. Engines operate best when air is cold, and therefore more dense and oxygen rich. The higher the engine space temperature rises, the more the efficiency is lost and this is typically in the 10-15% range. The efficiency can be improved by the installation of an air inlet ducted to the engine air inlet, which provides cool external air. In addition to air inlet ducting, the installation of an extraction fan to the engine space to remove the hot air created by the engine is recommended.

3. THE COOLING SYSTEM

The cooling system controls the overall operating temperature of the engine, and proper heat transfer is essential. There are three ways of cooling a marine diesel: direct seawater cooling, indirect or inter-cooling, and keel cooling.

What is direct cooling?

Raw seawater is drawn directly through the hull scoop and grating, seacock, and through a strainer. The raw water pump circulates the seawater through the engine block to cool it, after which it either exits straight overboard in a dry exhaust boat, or through the exhaust line in a wet exhaust installation. The engine will have a thermostat to bypass cooling water until the engine warms up. There are few direct seawater-cooled engines around and new ones are limited to smaller rated engines.

What is indirect cooling?

The indirect or inter-cooled engine has a seawater (SW) system and a freshwater (FW) system. The engine FW system is a closed loop system that uses a pump to circulate the water from the expansion tank, through the various engine water galleries, to carry heat away through the cooler or heat exchanger, and back to the expansion tank. The heat exchanger provides the interchange for transferring engine heat from the FW to the SW coolant. The SW is drawn from outside via the water scoop and grating and through the SW inlet valve, the strainer, to the suction side of the SW pump. The pressurized water is then pumped to the cooler, where it passes through the cooler tubes and transfers heat from the FW. The SW may be injected into the exhaust line and discharged overboard through the exhaust outlet. The freshwater cooling system must remain salt-water contamination-free to prevent corrosion or formation of sludge and scale that may impede coolant flow. This also reduces heat transfer rates by coating the engine block water passages with insulating scale build-up. This will result in gradual overheating, with all the damage that comes from it. Inhibitors must be maintained at the correct concentrations for performance, and to avoid damage.

What is keel cooling?

A keel cooling system is similar to the indirect cooling system except that the external seawater system is replaced with a closed loop system. This comprises a hull-mounted radiator that allows heat transfer to the surrounding water.

About the water intake scoop

The water intake scoop is designed so that when under way the water is forced into the water intake, creating positive pressure. This scoop is a cast fitting that has a filter or strainer over it to prevent weed and other material to penetrate. The scoop is always installed facing forward in a motorboat. In a sailing boat the scoop is installed facing to the rear so that water is not forced into the system when sailing. If a water pump impeller is leaking, water can work through and fill the exhaust line and ultimately the engine internal exhaust. The average small marine diesel requires approximately 2 pints (1 liter) of water per HP per minute (1.2 l/kW/min) and the scoop assists in achieving this. The strainers on the scoop are prone to fouling with material and barnacles and it is good practice to examine and clean them regularly to avoid starving the engine of cooling water. This is very common and the biggest enemy is plastic bags or parts of bags. When painting or applying antifouling, make sure you don't coat the grills too thickly or reduce the opening.

About the seacock or shutoff valve

The seacock is the main valve isolating the flow or supply of seawater from the sea through the hull to the cooling water system. Some seacocks have an integral strainer and filter on the outside. The seacock must be positioned correctly. If fitted too far outboard the suction can be lost or some aeration can occur. The result can be a water pump impeller running dry, and being damaged.

About cooling water strainers

Most strainers are made of plastic. Bronze strainers are still around but not as common now, and there are also custom stainless units. They are installed in the seawater suction line above the waterline, so that removal doesn't end up flooding the boat. It is always good practice to close the seacock before servicing the strainer, but don't forget to reopen it. The strainer housings have a clear plastic cover to allow easy inspection. The cover comes off and the strainer cage or element lifts out for cleaning. The top cover has a seal that consists of a nitrile O-ring. Always tighten the lid properly to prevent air getting sucked in by the pump. When replacing the cover, coat the seal with Vaseline, not grease.

About the system hoses and clamps

Seawater inlet hoses should be wire-reinforced. The flexible piping installation must avoid any excessive bend radius or kink. Always install *two* stainless steel hose clamps at each connection and tighten properly. Piping can collapse and cause intermittent overheating. This often happens at higher running speeds and increased engine compartment temperatures. It is good practice to regularly examine hoses for hardening or pinhole leaks.

What does the header or expansion tank do?

Water when heated expands, and when cooled, contracts. The expansion tank allows this to happen. The tank should be kept at the level recommended for your engine.

About the seawater pump

The raw or seawater pump is critical to the performance of the cooling system. It is usually a centrifugal pump that is gear-driven off the engine. The pump impeller is made of neoprene rubber. The impeller blades, or vanes, are lubricated by the water. Monitor telltale holes. A drip means that the seals are failing. Regular inspection and programmed replacement are recommended. Changing impellers every season or a maximum of around 500 hours is a good reliability measure. Carry several spare impellers in your kit.

About the freshwater pump

The freshwater pump is also critical to the performance of the cooling system. It is usually a centrifugal pump-belt, driven off the engine, and is relatively reliable. The pump impeller is made of neoprene rubber. Again monitor the telltale holes for leakage. Regular inspection and programmed replacement are recommended. Also check the rubber V-belts; excessive tension will cause bearing failure in pumps.

How to inspect a water pump impeller

When temperatures are high, the impeller may be fatigued. Follow this simple change procedure. Make sure that the cover screws are easy to open and lubricated.

1. Remove the pump cover, taking care that you do not damage the gasket.

2. Carefully pry out the impeller with a screwdriver or some wooden dowels on each side.

3. Check the impeller for damage, cracks, and flexibility.

4. Replace or fix the impeller. Coat it with grease or Vaseline.

5. Refit gasket and pump cover, but do not over-tighten the screws.

Water pump impeller troubleshooting

1. If there are pieces missing out of the blade tips at the center of the impeller, pitting at the ends, or the edges have a hollowed-out appearance, this is caused by cavitation. Cavitation is due to low pressures at the pump inlet and can be rectified by reducing inlet pipe restrictions and lengths, and increasing inlet pipe diameters.

2. If the impeller blade tips and end faces are worn, or the impeller drive is worn, this is also caused by cavitation, due to low pressures at the pump inlet. The same measures apply.

3. If the end faces of the impeller have a hard and polished appearance, or there are blades missing, this is caused by running the pump dry. The pump should not be run longer than 30 seconds with reduced fluids, and it should be stopped immediately if the fluids are gone.

4. If the impeller blades have excessive or permanent distortion or curving, this is caused by chemical action, excessive pump storage periods, or the end of the normal service life. Pumping incorrect fluids will have chemical effects. If an engine is stored for long periods or over a winter, removing the impeller is a good precaution.

5. If the impeller binds inside the pump housing, or the blades appear longer than the hub, or the impeller rubber is sticky and soft, this is caused by chemical actions, high fluid temperatures or long-term immersion. Pumps should be flushed clean after use, and drained if they are stored. High fluid temperatures should not be used.

6. If the impeller blades are cracked or parts of the blade are missing, this may be caused by the impeller reaching the end of its normal operational life. It may also be caused by high output pressures, and fluids of either high or low temperature. Running the pump dry can cause similar damage. Check and reduce pump pressures, or outlet pipe restrictions, such as long pipe runs or blockages.

What does the thermostat do?

The thermostat is essentially a heat-activated valve. It restricts the circulation of the engine coolant until the engine heats up to the nominal level. When the engine heats up, the thermostat opens to allow more water to circulate through the heat exchanger. A thermostat starts to open around 160°F (70°C) and is fully open at 185°F (85°C).

About the heat exchanger or cooler

The cooler transfers engine heat from the freshwater cooling circuit to the raw seawater system. The cooler tubes are prone to blockage through silt and scaling. Scaling can be reduced by idling for 10 minutes before stopping the engine, to cool it down.

About cooler zincs or anodes

The sacrificial anode or zinc is used to control corrosion. It should be removed and checked or replaced every 200 hours.

How to inspect and clean coolers

The following essential maintenance tasks should be completed regularly, and will maintain optimum performance. When temperatures cannot be maintained, coolers need to be opened, inspected and cleaned. To do the task you need a soft wire brush and a soft metal rod (copper or brass).

1. Close any isolation valves.

2. Drain the cooler.

3. Remove the cooler end bonnets.

4. Clean all accessible parts with a soft wire brush.

5. Push the rod through each tube. This should be slightly smaller than the tubes. In severe cases of fouling, acid cleaning may be required.

6. Flush the cooler and tubes well with fresh water.

7. Inspect and renew the gaskets and seals if damaged.

8. Re-assemble the cooler.

9. Run the engine up to normal speed and observe oil and water temperatures. Inspect for leaks.

Why are coolant additives used?

A number of additives are used in coolants to improve the performance. Coolant water must be chemically pure and should be either de-ionized, or distilled and demineralized. Additives are used to protect against cylinder liner erosion and pitting, boil-over, and to create a stable and non-corrosive system environment. This will offer protection and long life for the internal metal parts of the system, hoses, gaskets and seals. Coolant water may have sulfates, chlorides, dissolved solids and calcium. Additives can reduce vapor bubble formation by depositing a protective film on the cylinder liner surfaces, which acts as a barrier against collapsing vapor bubbles. Do not use general auto-type coolant additives. Make sure they are recommended for use on your diesel. Some additives may contain high silicate concentrations that can cause engine damage.

What about antifreeze protection?

Coolant should also have an antifreeze additive to prevent freezing and engine damage in cold climates. Most ethylene glycol based antifreeze solutions contain the required inhibitors for normal operation. Using only ethylene glycol antifreeze without inhibitors is not enough protection for your engine.

What is a corrosion inhibitor?

These water-soluble chemical compounds protect the metallic surfaces within the system against corrosion. Compounds can include borates, chromates and nitrites. Soluble oil should not be used as a corrosion inhibitor. Use only non-chromate inhibitors. Perform checks every 600 hours of operation, using test strips. The general levels allowed are as follows:

1. Chlorides–40ppm

2. Sulfates–100ppm

3. Total dissolved solids–350ppm max

4. Total hardness–170ppm max

5. pH level–5.5 to 9.0

4. THE LUBRICATING OIL SYSTEM

Lubricating oil separates the various engine working surfaces to prevent metal-to-metal contact. The pistons must receive adequate oil supplies to prevent expansion and seizure, caused by excess heat from increased friction on a dry cylinder wall. Oil has the dual function of lubricating the engine's moving parts and the removal of heat generated during the combustion process and friction. Oil removes heat from the outside of cylinder liners, heat from the pistons and inner walls of liners and cools the main bearings. Oil also carries away metal particles to the sump and oil filter. It acts as corrosion inhibitor on metal surfaces, and it allows the piston rings to form a seal and maintain compression.

How does oil circulate?

Oil is taken to the oil pump from a submerged suction in the oil sump or pan. Oil pumps are usually a 2-stage, positive displacement, gear-type pump. They are driven off the timing gear train to maintain a constant oil flow. A constant volume of oil is pumped, although flow will decrease slightly with increasing pressure. A non-adjustable pressure regulator valve is installed on the pump outlet side. A simple bypass valve is usually installed to limit the maximum oil pressure. This valve will divert excess oil back to the sump. The pressurized oil is passed though the oil filter, then distributed around the various oil galleries and points within the engine. As oil reaches the crankcase bearings, flow is restricted, and the pump forces oil into the clearances between the main bearings and crankshaft. Oil is carried to the crank, connecting rod bearings, main and connecting rod journals. Oil may also be used in turbo bearings and sometimes under piston crowns. Liner, piston and rings are lubricated by oil thrown by the camshaft and crankshaft. The oil manifold supplies oil to the governor and rocker gear. Oil usually flows off the end of the rocker arms to lubricate valve springs and stems. Oil also lubricates the timing gear bearings. The oil returns via gravity back to the sump. In many engines, the heat is dissipated through the oil cooler and through oil sump surfaces.

About oil filtration

All oils contain contaminants and the content levels must be minimized. These may be metals, fibers, microbial growth. Most damage is caused by hard particles that are slightly larger than the clearance of contact surfaces. Critical sizes are 0.5 to 45 microns and usually greater than 3-5 microns. Oil filters will remove these abrasive materials and contaminants. The oil lubricant provides a strong film between all working surfaces and reduces engine wear. Oil films typically have a thickness of around 0.08 mm between the shaft and bearings, and the film must be strong enough to prevent surface to surface contact.

What causes oil contamination?

In a 4-stroke diesel engine, oil reduces engine wear, and absorbs contaminants that enter the engine. Most contaminants are expelled from the engine with exhaust gasses. Some remain in the cylinders and crankcase to corrode metal parts and form sludge and lacquer deposits. Most events that occur in the engine have an effect on the oil. When injection and combustion pressures are raised, the load increases on the pistons and bearings. Excess oil will bypass pistons and rings into the combustion chamber where it burns forming carbon deposits. Oil is affected by chemical composition, the presence of nitrogen, phosphor, potassium, sulfur, and external growth factors, such as temperature, pH values, water and oxygen. Oil neutralizes the acids that form, and breaks up the deposits caused by combustion blow-by. Oil cleans by dissolving the sulfur that is converted to acid when the fuel is burned. High oil temperatures cause the chemical breakdown of oil, so maintaining engine temperatures is essential. The effect of acid formation can be reduced by operating the engine at the proper working temperatures. Humidity in combustion air also assists in acid formation.

All about oil standards

It is essential that the correct grades of oil be used for the pre-vailing temperature conditions, and that the filter be changed regularly along with the oil. The nominal rating of oil viscosity must be maintained if correct lubrication is to be achieved. This is dependent on the engine remaining within the proper operat-ing temperature ranges. Engine oil should comply with API CC/CD specifications, and may be synthetic, mineral, or blended. Mineral oils have various additives, and they are more suited to infrequent use or less demanding service such as boats. Oils in generators are changed at 500 hours and synthetic oils usually last 10 times longer. This results in a cleaner engine, rings and liners and increases engine life by 40%, and lube oil consumption decreases by 75%. SAE standards match oil viscosity to operat-ing temperatures. The W notation is the winter service rating defined at 0°F.

Engine Oil Viscosity

Viscosity	Temperature
SAE 10W	-10°F to 70°F
SAE 30	+20°F to 100°F
SAE 40	+45°F to 120°F
SAE 10W-30	-10°F to +100°F
SAE 15W-40	+5°F to 120°F

About oil additives

Oil contains hundreds of chemical compounds and often additives to improve its lubrication characteristics. Oil additives allow continuous operation at high speed, or at raised engine temperatures. Oils have oxidation inhibitors and antioxidants to prevent oil thickening and formation of varnish and sludge that can seize fuel pump plungers. Anti-foaming agents are used to minimize foam formation, which can cause a loss of oil pressure and a loss of lubrication. Air bubbles in oil will retain heat and the cooling ability will be greatly reduced. Detergents are used to prevent combustion by-products from adhering to metal surfaces, as deposits also lead to excessive wear. Dispersal compounds such as calcium and barium prevent smaller particles within the oil agglomerating to form larger ones that can cause damage, block oil galleries and passages. They keep particles suspended in the oil, which can be filtered out. Zinc and phosphorus act as lubricants to resist pressure inside cylinders. Magnesium inhibits excess wear and corrosion. Additives deplete in normal engine operation and require renewal. Remember that the longer an oil is used, the greater the oxidation, which alters the viscosity. Alkaline additives are sometimes called buffers and they prevent acid corrosion and wear on the internal engine parts. The alkalinity of oil is referred to as Total Base Number (TBN) and the higher the TBN the greater the ability of the oil to neutralize acids.

What causes oil problems?

Problems that can occur are as follows:

1. **Fuel in Oil.** Fuel in oil can create a crankcase explosion risk and is characterized by low lube oil viscosity.

2. **Water in Oil.** Water in the oil will cause emulsification and destroy the lubrication properties. The system must be completely flushed out after a leak repair and no moisture allowed to remain.

How does microbe growth occur?

Where water and oxygen are present, microbiotic growth within the oil and system can occur. Anaerobic micro-organisms can live in oxygen-free areas on partly mineralized hydrocarbons, and oil additives can stimulate growth of organisms. As the oil degrades the oil characteristics change, caused not only by the degradation but by the organisms that produce extracellular biopolymers (slime), usually bacteria and fungi, and by yeast contamination. Organisms start to produce surfactants and biopolymers when in contact with a hydrophobic culture medium (oil), which they can break down. This leads to increased exposure and oil break-down, and the optimum temperature range is 3° - 40°C. Once the system is infected, considerable flushing is required.

Why do you perform oil testing?

With larger boats and engines, it makes sense to take oil samples at regular intervals for oil analysis. All leading oil companies offer this service. The analysis of the various trace metals found in the sample are good indicators of wear. Results can be obtained via Internet with some companies. Different parts of an engine have different metals all washed by lube oil. Oils are analyzed using a spectrograph. As each element is burnt in an electric arc, the sample emits a unique light frequency. The test results show amounts of each metal present in parts per million (ppm), and spectrochemical analysis is given in parts per million by weight. The analyst looks for wear metals contaminants and oil additives. Regular intervals of oil analysis, not just a single test, are important for trend analysis. Wear metals have differing thresholds, indicating that problems are developing. Sharp increases in wear metals, or a major shift in physical properties, signal impending problems.

Taking oil samples

The oil sample must be taken uniformly as wear metals are heavy and sink to the bottom of the oil sump, if oil is settled. Take the oil sample within 20 minutes of engine shutdown, so that the oil material is equally dispersed in suspension. Do not sample from the sump bottom but from a point before the oil filter or suction, or out of the dipstick tube. Drop the suction hose to the sump bottom, then raise it an inch for the sample.

Reading the results

New engines will show higher wear metal numbers than old engines, and baselines are best established after the engine is worn in. On analysis reports, "normal" status indicates that the physical properties of the lubricant are within acceptable limits, and no signs of excessive contamination or wear are present. "Monitor" status indicates that specific test results are outside acceptable ranges, but not serious enough to confirm abnormal conditions. Initial abnormalities often indicate the same result patterns as temporary overloading or extended operations. "Abnormal" status indicates that lubricant physical properties, contaminations or component wear are unsatisfactory but not critical. "Critical" status is serious enough to warrant immediate diagnostic and corrective action to prevent major long-term performance loss or in-service failure.

What do the elements mean?

There are typically 21 different elements present in lubricating oil. A simple test method is a viscosity test using a viscosity test stick. The new and used oil must be allowed to stand for an hour and stabilize at room temperature. The test stick is angled so that each oil sample runs down a channel. When the new oil reaches a mid-scale point the position of the used oil is read. If the used oil has not reached the same point, it has a high viscosity, usually due to oxidation or high insolubles. If the oil has run past the scale point the additives may be failing, or there may be fuel oil contamination. These test kits should be part of any testing regime; they are simple and easy to perform.

Engine Oil Analysis

Element	Indicators
Iron	High levels indicate wear from rings, shafts, gears, valve trains, cylinder walls, pistons or liners
Chromium	May indicate excessive wear of chromed parts such as rings, liners and some additives
Nickel	Secondary indicator of wear from some bearings, shafts, valves and valve guides
Aluminum	Wear from pistons, rod bearings, and certain shaft types
Lead	An overlay on main rods and bearings
Copper	Wear from bearings, rocker arm bushings, pin bushings, thrust washers, and other brass bronze parts
Tin	Wear from bearings and pistons in some engines
Silver	Wear of bearings. A secondary indicator of oil cooler problems, when coolant is detected
Titanium	Used as an alloy in steel for gears and bearings
Silicon	Airborne dust/dirt contamination indicates poor air cleaner servicing, and can accelerate wear
Boron	A coolant additive, and additive in some oils
Sodium	A coolant additive, and additive in some oils
Potassium	A coolant additive
Molybdenum	Wear from rings, and additive in some oils
Phosphorus	Antirust agents and combustion chamber deposit reducers

Zinc	An anti-oxidant, corrosion inhibitor, anti-wear additive, detergent and extreme pressure additive
Calcium	A detergent, dispersant and acid neutralizer
Barium	Corrosion inhibitors, detergents and rust inhibitors
Magnesium	Dispersant and detergent additive and alloying metal
Antimony	A bearing overlay alloy or oil additive
Vanadium	A heavy fuel contaminant

5. THE AIR SYSTEM

In a normally aspirated engine, the air for fuel combustion is drawn in through an air filter and then compressed. The amount of fuel that can be burnt within a cylinder, and therefore the power of the engine, are limited by the air mass within each cylinder. If insufficient air is available for proper combustion, the engine will not reach the required speed. The governor controlling fuel injection will try and give more power and inject more fuel. This generally results in the creation of black smoke. Air starvation is caused by several factors. The air filter may be clogged, although on marine diesels this is not common. The air filter in a marine engine may trap salt. A common cause of air starvation is inadequate air to the compartment, either from bad design or covered inlet vents. Some boats have a dedicated supply fan.

What is turbocharging?

The options to increase the air supply are to pre-cool the air to increase the air density, or to use turbocharging. Turbocharging increases the available power output for the same normally aspirated engine. Turbocharging raises the air density by increasing the pressure at which the cylinder is filled with air during the air intake stroke. This has the effect of increasing the engine power for the same cylinder size. The turbocharger is essentially a small air compressor driven by a turbine in the exhaust line. As the engine load increases, the hot exhaust gas output velocity increases, which increases the turbine speed to drive the air compressor faster, which raises the air pressure into the cylinders. As the air is compressed into the engine cylinders, the air temperature also increases. This reduces the available oxygen, so some engines may have intercoolers installed. These cool the compressed air, which improves the combustion.

What is an intercooler or aftercooler?

This is a cooler installed within the air inlet side of a turbocharger. Cooling air will raise the air density, further increasing the effectiveness of the turbocharger. The cooler is water cooled to maximize heat transfer rates.

Turbocharger troubleshooting

Turbocharger faults cause reductions in the engine power output, generate black exhaust smoke and increase oil consumption. The turbo shaft assembly should be inspected where possible to assist in determining the fault. This requires the removal of the inlet and exhaust trunk. The turbine should be rotated by hand and the housing should be examined for signs of contact or rubbing. The oil drain should be checked and cleaned if fouled, and signs of oil leaks should also be investigated. Engines subject to low speeds or extended idle periods tend to leak and this usually disappears when the engine is loaded up.

Failure causes in turbochargers

The most common cause of turbocharger failure is hot shutdown. When an engine is shutdown suddenly, the turbo continues to rotate without oil, and turbo life is reduced from a lack of lubrication. Eventually bearing wear allows the housing to contact the turbine, and out-of-balance conditions result, with serious damage or destruction. When stopping an engine it is good practice to operate at slow speeds for a few minutes to allow the turbocharger to spool down, and for cooling to take place. Never rev the engine and then shutdown as the turbo will be rotating without lubrication and this may damage the bearings. Turbochargers rotate at very high speeds and generally use engine oil for lubrication, so maintaining clean oil is essential.

Why is the turbocharger so noisy?

Turbochargers tend to make serious noises when something is wrong or degraded.

1. Restricted or clogged air inlet filters.

2. The rotating turbine assembly is binding or touching the housing.

3. The flanges on the manifolds are loose, creating leaks.

4. There is an object inside the compressor housing, inlet ducting, or the manifold.

Why is the turbine assembly binding?

1. There may have been ingress of material causing turbine or compressor damage.

2. The turbine or compressor wheel is contacting the housing due to bearing wear or failure.

3. There is an accumulation of carbon deposits in the turbine housing or on the turbine blades.

Why are the seals leaking?

1. There are restricted or clogged air inlet filters.

2. The oil drain lines are clogged.

3. The crankcase breather is clogged.

4. The bearings are worn or failing.

5. There is a piston ring leakage or high crankcase pressures.

6. The compressor wheel is damaged.

6. THE EXHAUST SYSTEM

Stringent emissions legislation is now being introduced and be-coming mandatory in many parts of the world. It is inevitable that some fuel will remain unburned after combustion, and come out in the exhaust. Maintenance is essential to reduce this to a minimum. The exhaust engine noise is caused by the explosion during combustion. The shock waves resonate and echo through the cylinder and reverberate through the exhaust. Smoke color can be indicative of problems; normal exhaust has little or no color.

What are the parts of the exhaust system?

The basic exhaust system comprises the engine exhaust manifold; the water injection elbow; the exhaust hoses; the waterlock; the muffler; the gooseneck and the transom exhaust outlet. Manu-facturers such as Vetus offer good advice on the various configu-rations and parts required to install a proper exhaust system.

Fig. 6-1 Exhaust System Installation
Courtesy of Vetus

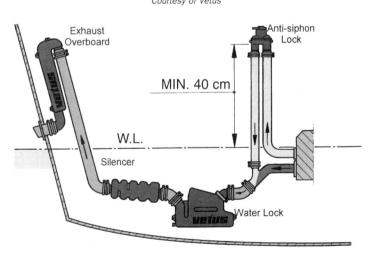

Why do you have a wet exhaust?

Exhaust gas can reach over 1100°F (600°C) on a diesel engine. When the water is injected into the exhaust line, the high temperature is reduced significantly. This reduces both the pressure and volume. The exhaust gas speed is diminished, reducing the exhaust noise level. The temperature reduction allows the use of rubber compounds. The heat radiates less to surrounding areas and materials. When the gases mix with the water, much of the particles within the exhaust are captured making the exhaust emission much cleaner. In general, to ensure proper drainage of wet exhaust systems, the pipe from the injection point to the exhaust must be installed with a consistent downward angle along the entire exhaust length.

About the injection or mixing elbow

The mixing elbow is at the exit point from the engine. In many cases the seawater is directly fed from the engine seawater supply into the elbow. In some cases the water injection point is below the waterline, or less than 6 inches (15 cm) above the waterline when the boat is heeled. This creates the danger of water siphoning back into the engine when the engine is stopped, or when the boat is heeled. In this case, an anti-siphon lock or air vent in the line, above the waterline, should be installed. The vent line always goes to the transom, well above the waterline.

A warning on wet exhausts

Waterlocks are used to prevent water going back to the engine. When a lot of starting attempts are made with a diesel engine, starting may become more difficult as water builds up within the waterlock and silencer. Some water remains from the previous operation. At these start attempts, some water is injected as the engine turns over without any exhaust pressure to blow it out. This excess water can be drained off from the small valves located at the bottom of the waterlock.

About anti-siphon vents

Air vents with internal valve assemblies are prone to blockages from salt crystal formations. They should be examined as part of the boat maintenance routine. The vents should be removed and soaked in fresh water to dissolve salt crystals, and to rinse dirt and corrosion particles. Vetus recommends to coat the valve assembly with a Teflon spray or silicon oil before reassembly to ensure good operation.

What does the silencer or muffler do?

The silencer is a moulded plastic chamber that allows exhaust gases to expand and have less volume and therefore reduce the exhaust noise. They are moulded so that they create a swirling action of the water to reduce exhaust noise. These should be mounted as close as possible to a vertical position. The installation of a silencer is important and manufacturer's instructions must be followed carefully. In general when installed on a sailboat the silencer should be as close to a midship position as possible, to prevent water flowing into the engine when the boat heels. The silencer inlet point must remain below the exhaust injection elbow at all times.

What does the waterlock do?

In a wet exhaust, once the engine stops, there will be some water remaining in the exhaust line. It must not be allowed to drain back to the engine where it would cause serious damage. The waterlock, also called a water lift muffler, or water trap, stops this flow by capturing and retaining it. When the engine next starts, the water is ejected and you will often see a sizeable spurt of water at start up. The waterlock is usually a moulded plastic chamber installed lower than the engine and exhaust outlet, so that all water drains down to it.

What does the gooseneck do?

The gooseneck is often installed adjacent to the transom exhaust outlet. In some boats, the hose is looped up with the top of the loop at least 16 inches (40 cm) above the waterline. In smaller boats this clearance may not be possible in the small space under a cockpit floor. The solution is to install a moulded plastic gooseneck that prevents and captures any water ingress. The gooseneck also has a secondary muffler function.

About exhaust hoses and clamps

Hoses usually consist of a multi-layer rubber compound with steel spiral reinforcing. The exterior is of rough appearance and impervious to fuel, salt water, etc. It is very smooth internally, to reduce resistance and resultant back pressure. Approved hoses are rated at temperatures in the range of minus 100°F (40°C) to plus 212°F (100°C). Exhaust hoses should fit neatly onto the various components such as the waterlock and mufflers. Do not use oil or grease to slide them on, only use water or soap as a lubricant. Always use *two* stainless steel clamps on every connection and ensure they are tight. Always properly secure or support all parts of the exhaust system, including the hose, as they must contain the added weight of water within them.

Why do you need a transom exhaust outlet flap?

The flap is a hinged assembly that is closed when the engine is off and opens under exhaust gas pressure. This prevents water from following seas from surging back into the exhaust line.

What causes blue-white smoke?

Blue-white smoke appears during cold starting. When the temperature is too low to burn the fuel, smoke is created by unburned fuel vapor, indicating a lack of ignition. As the engine warms up, the smoke will turn blue. Continuing blue smoke indicates worn or stuck piston rings, injector leaks, piston cracks, worn cylinder liners or valve guides. The unburned fuel particles are then exhausted and usually have a rich fuel smell. Another cause of white smoke at engine start up is faulty glowplugs or glowplug system. A low engine cranking speed can create an excessive amount of white smoke. Once the engine is up to normal operating temperature, a faulty injector can cause white smoke. Other problems include timing problems, low engine compression, an injection pump, or air in the fuel system.

What causes black or gray smoke?

Black or gray smoke is caused by soot. It indicates an improper air to fuel ratio and incomplete combustion; high exhaust back pressure; restricted air inlets; turbocharger malfunction; fuel injector problems; timing faults; engine overloads or low compression.

7. ENGINE OPERATION AND MAINTENANCE

There are certain points to consider when operating diesel engines; this also applies to diesel generators.

1. **Warming.** Operate at 1200 rpm or less for 1-2 minutes, and extend this to 3-4 minutes in cold weather. Allow the engine sufficient time to reach normal operating temperature and for parts to expand.

2. **Oil Pressure.** Stop engine if oil pressure does not rise in 5 seconds and find out why.

3. **Idling.** Do not let the engine run on light or no load for periods exceeding 5-10 minutes. This causes cylinder glazing and deposits within the engine, which increases maintenance costs. Prolonged idling causes the coolant temperature to fall below normal range. Crankcase oil dilution can then occur due to incomplete fuel combustion. This results in the formation of gummy deposits on valves, pistons, piston rings, and promotes rapid accumulation of engine sludge and unburned fuel in exhaust system.

4. **Cooling Water.** Always visually check the seawater overboard discharge after starting to ensure that coolant is passing through the engine. If the water is not coming out of the exhaust, or out of overboard discharge, stop the engine and investigate immediately. Don't wait for the high temperature alarm and possible damage. Don't allow the pump to run dry, or the engine to overheat.

5. **Stopping.** Operate the engine for 5-10 minutes and allow temperatures to come down evenly. Avoid revving the engine prior to stopping as this will affect the lubrication of moving parts, such as turbochargers.

Engine lay-up tasks

1. Run engine until warm, then drain and replace the oil. Also change the filter. Drain and replace the transmission oil when warm. To avoid condensation, top the oil right up.

2. Top up the fuel tank, add biocide and stabilizer to the fuel, then circulate the treated fuel and check for leaks. Drain any water within the filter/separator bowl.

3. Clean the seawater strainer. Rinse the seawater system with fresh water to dilute salt if possible.

4. Treat the coolant with antifreeze, and run the engine to circulate it properly.

5. Lubricate the throttle and gear change linkages using light machine oil.

6. Tape over the exhaust outlet using duct tape.

Engine spring maintenance tasks

1. Change the oil before the start of the season or at the end of the lay-up period, including the oil filters. Run the engine, put it in gear and add some load against the mooring lines. Run up to normal operating temperature.

2. Operate the transmission and throttle cables over the full range several times and lubricate them.

3. Check and clean the seawater strainer.

4. Check the engine mounts, clean and tighten.

5. Check the electrical connections, clean and tighten.

About engine maintenance

Maintenance should always be carried out in accordance with the engine manufacturer's recommendations. I have been extensively involved in preparing and implementing planned maintenance programs on commercial and offshore vessels. Good maintenance will significantly reduce machinery down time, and overall operating costs. A good maintenance schedule, properly recorded, may have significant benefits on the resale value of the boat.

What to do daily or weekly

1. Check the lube oil level and top up as required

2. Check the fuel oil pre-filter for water and drain as required

3. Check coolant water level and top up as required

4. Check transmission oil level and top up as required

5. Visual inspection for fuel, oil and water leaks

6. Check and top up batteries

What to do every 150 hours/monthly

1. Check the fuel filter and replace as required

2. Check the air filter

3. Check and clean the crankcase breathers

4. Perform lube oil analysis

5. Check water system anodes if installed

6. Check and drain water tanks of water

7. Check and clean seawater strainers

8. Open and close all valves 5 times to exercise them

What to do every 250 hours/3 months

1. Change the engine oil
2. Change the oil filter
3. Check the condition of seawater pump impeller
4. Check and change transmission oil

What to do every 500 hours/12 months

1. Check and clean the crankcase vent tube
2. Inspect all air intake hoses, hose connections
3. Open and clean water coolers
4. Check and re-tension rubber drive belt
5. Check and tighten the alternator mounting bolts
6. Check the coolant water additives
7. Check and tighten all coupling bolts
8. Check engine cable harness for chafe
9. Tighten starter and alternator connections
10. Tighten engine negative connections
11. Check the condition of the coolant filler cap

What to do every 1000 hours/24 months

1. Check the engine crankshaft vibration damper
2. Perform a pressure test of the cooling system
3. Check that the engine mountings are clean and tight
4. Replace the water pump impeller

What to do every 2000 hours

1. Check and adjust the valve clearances

2. Flush the cooling system and add new coolant

3. Have all injectors and fuel pumps checked and overhauled

8. ENGINE TROUBLESHOOTING

Injectors can be the source of trouble when the engine has high operating hours and an increase in smoke has been noticed, or the engine has been running rough. Injectors typically have a reduction in opening pressure, and this can be 200 to 300 psi. When this is exceeded, injectors may require resetting. Injectors may have poor atomization or be blocked if they have not been serviced for a long period. Air in the fuel system may be a problem, especially in engines that have not been started for long periods. Check that the fuel filters are not clogged or full of water. Where some water may have passed through, the addition of a fuel lubricant additive to free up metering valves and plungers may solve the problem. Engine timing and low compression problems can occur on engines with high operating hours. In some cases, poor fuel quality may be the only cause.

The engine cranks but will not start

1. Incorrect starting procedure

2. Fuel supply valve closed

3. Fuel filter clogged

4. Fuel lift pump may have a fault

5. Exhaust restricted

6. Fuel filter plugged or full water

7. Injection pump not getting fuel

8. Air in the fuel system

9. Faulty injection pump or nozzles

The engine has a low cranking speed

1. Air in the fuel system

2. Exhaust restricted

3. Fuel pressure low with a possible fuel pump fault

4. Injector fault

The engine is hard to start

1. Gearbox engaged

2. Air in the fuel line; it needs bleeding

3. Starter motor speed low; battery has low voltage

4. Water or dirt in the fuel system

5. Air filter element clogged

6. Injection nozzles clogged or dirty

The engine starts and then stops

1. Fuel filter element clogged

2. Air in the fuel line; it needs bleeding

3. Injection nozzles clogged or dirty

4. Engine timing problem

The engine has a lack of power

1. Air intake restricted or clogged element

2. Engine fuel filter or pre-filter clogged

3. Engine overheating

4. Engine temperature too low, check the thermostat

5. Valve clearances out of spec

6. Dirty or faulty injection nozzles

7. Injection pump timing is out

8. Turbocharger fault

9. Leak in the exhaust manifold gasket

10. Fuel line restriction

The engine has a loss of compression

1. Worn piston

2. Worn or broken piston rings

3. Excess cylinder wear

4. Leaking valves

5. Leaking or blown head gasket

The engine has a high temperature

1. No cooling water, faulty water pump impeller

2. Water pump rubber V-belt loose or broken

3. Coolant level low, check for possible hose leaks

4. Seawater strainer clogged with debris

5. Lube oil level low

6. Air cleaner filter clogged

7. One of the injector pumps faulty

8. Thermostat faulty

9. Heat exchanger tubes clogged

10. Coolant water cap faulty

The engine has a low temperature

1. Thermostat faulty

2. High oil pressure

3. Restriction in the relief valve oil passage

4. Relief valve out of adjustment

The engine has a low oil pressure

1. Lube oil level low

2. Lube oil filter element clogged

3. Oil pump faulty

4. Bearing problem

5. Oil pump suction filter screen clogged

6. Oil relief valve malfunctioning

7. Air leak in the oil pump suction line

8. Oil pump gears very worn or damaged

9. Oil pump cover loose

10. Oil pump gaskets leaking

11. Oil pressure gauge faulty

The engine is using too much oil

1. System oil leaks at joints

2. Crankcase vent may be dirty or clogged

3. Incorrect oil viscosity

4. Air cleaner may be clogged

The exhaust smoke color is black/gray

1. Engine has low compression

2. Injector pump fault

3. Injector nozzles dirty or faulty

4. Exhaust line has a restriction

5. Leak in the head gasket

6. Engine timing problem

7. Turbocharger problem or leaking seal

8. Fuel quality substandard

The exhaust smoke color is white

1. Engine cold, low temperature

2. Valve stuck

3. Engine has low compression

4. Leak in the head gasket

5. Thermostat may be malfunctioning

6. Injector nozzles clogged

7. Engine timing problem

The engine is knocking

1. Engine starting to overheat
2. Fuel supply problems
3. Engine coolant level low
4. Engine thermostat faulty
5. Fuel filter element clogged
6. Water, dirt or air in the fuel system
7. Injector nozzles dirty or faulty
8. Engine oil level is low
9. Fuel injection pump timing is out

There is high fuel consumption

1. Air filter clogged
2. Engine overloaded
3. Valve clearances incorrect
4. Injection nozzles dirty
5. Engine timing fault
6. Faulty turbocharger
7. Engine temperature low, thermostat faulty

The engine is misfiring

1. Turbocharger defective
2. Engine temperature too low
3. Engine oil level low
4. Injector either clogged or faulty
5. Injection pump timing problem
6. Cooling water temperature low

9. ENGINE STARTING SYSTEMS

The systems that make up a typical electrical system include the battery; the engine control panel; the wiring loom; the preheating system; the starter motor and solenoid; shut-down solenoids; instrument sensors and transducers, and the alternator. There is a basic sequence of electrical functions that take place when starting the engine. When the key switch is turned to <ON>, this closes the circuit to supply voltage to the control circuit, and generally initiates alarms. When no audible or visual alarms occur, no power is on. When the key switch is turned to the <PREHEAT> position, this energizes the heating glowplugs or heating elements. When the key switch is turned to <START> or the engine <START> button is pressed, voltage is then applied to the starter motor solenoid coil. The solenoid pulls in to supply the main starting circuit current through a set of contacts. The contacts when closed supply current to the starter motor positive terminal. This turns over the starter motor to start the engine.

What is an electric engine starter?

Essentially the electric starter consists of a DC motor, a solenoid, and a pinion engaging drive. The DC motor is typically series wound. It provides the high initial torque required to overcome the friction and inertia (such as oil viscosity), and cylinder compression. The starter motor then accelerates the engine to a point where self-ignition temperatures are reached and combustion starts (typically in the range 60-200 rpm depending on whether glowplugs are used). The starter motor torque is transmitted by the pinion and ring gear on the flywheel. The drive gear pinion has a reduction gear of around 15:1.

What is the solenoid?

The solenoid is essentially a large high-current relay that consists of coil and armature, moving and fixed contacts. The solenoid is mounted directly to the starting motor housing, which reduces cables and interconnections to a minimum. When the solenoid coil is energized by the starting circuit, the solenoid plunger is drawn into the energized core and this closes the main contacts to supply current to the starter motor. On some starters, the solenoid also has a mechanical function. The solenoid activates a shift or engaging lever to slide the overrunning clutch along the shaft to mesh the pinion gear with the flywheel. When engaged, the starter motor then turns the engine, so meshing occurs before starting.

About the starter motor types

The motor consists of four poles shoes or magnets. Some motors use permanent magnets. The poles are fitted with an excitation winding which creates the magnetic field when current is applied. The rotating part, called the armature, also incorporates the commutator. The four carbon brushes provide the positive and negative power supply. There are four basic DC motor types in use, based on connection of the field windings. The field windings are connected either in series or parallel with the armature windings.

1. **Shunt (Parallel) Wound Motors.** The motor operates at a constant speed regardless of loads applied to it. It is the most common motor used in industrial applications and is suited to applications where starting torque conditions are not excessive.

2. **Permanent Magnet Excited Motors.** The permanent magnet starter offers the advantages of reduced weight, physical size and generates less heat than normal field type starters. Current is supplied via the brushes and commutator directly to the armature. Another feature is that a reduction gear is used, which allows faster speeds and increased torque.

3. **Series Wound Motors.** On this type of DC motor the speed varies according to the load applied. Speed increases with load decrease.

4. **Compound Motors (Series/Shunt Wound).** This configuration is often used on large starter motors. It combines the advantages of both shunt and series motors, and is used where high starting torques and constant speeds are required.

Fig. 9-1 Starter Motor

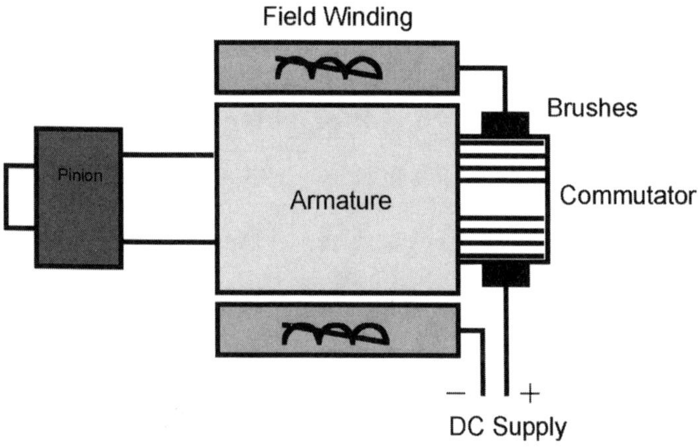

Field Winding

Pinion

Armature

Brushes

Commutator

$-$ $+$

DC Supply

What about pinion engaging drives?

The pinion engaging drive is located within the end shield assembly of the starter and consists of the pinion engaging drive and pinion, the overrunning clutch, the engagement lever or linkage and spring. When the motor operates, the drive gear meshes with the ring gear or flywheel teeth to turn the engine, and then disengages after starting. The overrunning clutch has two important functions, the first is to transmit the power from the motor to the pinion, and the second is to stop the starter motor armature from over-speeding and being damaged when the engine starts. Pre-engaged starters generally use a roller type clutch, while larger multi-plate types are used in sliding gear starters.

About starter types

There are several types of starters in use, the most common being the overrunning clutch starter, while the inertia-engagement Bendix drive is now less common. There are four basic groups of starter motors:

Pre-engaged (direct) drive starters

The most common type of starter motor is the solenoid-operated direct drive unit and the operating principles are the same for all solenoid-shifted starter motors. When the ignition switch is placed in the Start position, the control circuit energizes the pull-in and hold-in windings of the solenoid. The solenoid plunger moves and pivots the shift lever, which in turn locates the drive pinion gear and connects it with the engine flywheel. When the solenoid plunger is moved all the way, the contact disc closes the circuit from the battery to the starter motor. Current flows through the field coils and the armature. This develops the magnetic fields that cause the armature to rotate, thus turning the engine.

Gear reduction starters

Some manufacturers use a gear reduction starter to provide increased torque. The gear reduction starter differs from most other designs in that the armature does not drive the pinion directly. In this design, the armature drives a small gear that is in constant mesh with a larger gear. Depending on the application, the ratio between these two gears is between 2:1 and 3.5:1. The additional reduction allows a small motor to turn at higher speeds and greater torque with less current draw. The solenoid operation is similar to that of the solenoid-shifted direct drive starter in that the solenoid moves the plunger, which engages the starter drive.

Sliding gear drive starters

These two-stage starters have either mechanical or electrical pinion rotation. The electrical units have a two-stage electrical pinion-engaging drive. The first stage allows meshing of the starter pinion without cranking the engine over. The second stage starts when the pinion fully travels and meshes. This allows full excitation and current flow to the starter motor. The first stage of mechanical units has a solenoid switch, which pushes forward the pinion engaging drive via a lever. When pinion meshing occurs, current is applied to the starter via the solenoid switch.

Bendix drive inertia starter

The Bendix friction-clutch mechanism drive was developed in the early 20th century. It uses a drive friction clutch, which has a drive pinion mounted on a spiral-threaded sleeve. The sleeve rotates within the pinion, and moves the pinion outwards to mesh with the flywheel ring gear. The impact of this meshing action is absorbed by the friction clutch. The engine, once started, turns at a higher speed and drives the Bendix gear at a higher speed than the starter motor. The pinion then rotates in the opposite direction to the spiral shaft and disengages. A common fault is where the drive pinion is thrown out of mesh and then stops. Always wait several seconds before attempting to restart or the drive mechanism may be damaged. Another fault is when the pinion does not engage after the starting motor is energized, and a high-pitched whine is emitted from the starter. Turn off the ignition immediately as the unloaded DC starter motor will overspeed and be seriously damaged. Problems can be minimized by ensuring that the sleeve and pinion threads are clean and lubricated, so that the pinion engages and disengages freely. The Bendix gear, shaft, bearings and end plates can be cleaned of dried grease with WD40 and oiled with a fine sewing machine oil.

Starter maintenance

Starter installation is generally limited to two factors. The first is to make sure that it is mechanically secure, and the second is that the attached cables are of the correct rating and that terminal nuts are properly torqued so that they do not work loose. In addition, the negative cable should also be attached as close as possible to the starter. Starter motor design is generally robust as it must withstand the shocks of meshing, engine vibration, salt and moisture laden air, water, oil, temperature extremes, high levels of overload, etc. A common problem, especially on idle vessels, is the build up of surface corrosion, or accumulated dirt on the shaft and pinion gear assembly, and lack of lubrication causing seizure or failure to engage. It is good practice to remove the starter every 12 months, clean, and lightly oil the components according to the manufacturer's recommendations.

Problems often occur with seized brushes, primarily caused by lack of use. Always manually check that brushes are moving freely in the brush-holders, and that the commutator is clean. Remove all dust and particles using a vacuum cleaner. Wash out with a quality spray electrical cleaner if it is badly soiled. Follow the DC motor maintenance procedures. Do not clean or polish the commutator with any abrasive materials.

Starter troubleshooting

Many people are familiar with the loud click and then silence when the start solenoid operates but the starter fails to turn over. The main causes are a bad negative or positive connection, both caused by loose or dirty terminals. A solenoid plunger may also stick and not close fully, preventing the main contacts from closing.

About preheating glowplugs.

Some engines will not start without preheating. They often require extended engine starting turnover times which may overheat and damage the starter. Direct Injected (DI) engines commonly have glowplug heaters installed within each cylinder. They preheat the air in each cylinder to facilitate starting. In cold weather, this will dramatically decrease the electrical power requirements to start the engine.

1. **Activation.** Prior to engine starting, the plugs are activated for an operator-selected period, or interlocked to a timer, typically in the range of 15 to 20 seconds.

2. **Power Consumption.** The glowplugs can draw relatively large current levels for a short time. If your battery is low, allow a few seconds after preheating before starting as this enables the battery voltage to recover from the heater load.

About air intake heaters

These grid-resistor heaters are installed in the main air intake of DI engines and there is normally only one heating element.

What about preheating control

Many preheating circuits have relays, either timed or un-timed. Timed relays are often a common cause of failure. It is advisable to have a straight relay with a separate switch; simply preheat manually for 15 seconds, and then start the engine.

Pre-heater maintenance

Pre-heater glowplug connections must be regularly checked if they are to function properly. The connections must be cleaned, and tightened every six months. The insulation around the glow-plug connections must also be cleaned. It is a common fault to have oil and sediment tracking across to the engine block with a serious loss of preheating power. The glowplugs should be re-moved and cleaned yearly. Take care not to damage the heating element.

There is no preheating

1. Loss of power (fuse failure)

2. Connection fault on engine to first plug

3. Relay failure

4. Connection on ignition switch disconnected

5. Terminal short circuiting to engine block

There is partial preheating

1. One or more glowplug failed

2. Glowplug interconnection failure

3. Dirt around glowplug causing tracking

Engine starting system diagrams

Always check the electrical diagrams supplied in the operator's manual for your specific engine model. Make sure that you have the correct circuit diagram for the installed engine. It is a good idea to laminate a copy in plastic to have a working copy ready to use when troubleshooting. The table gives some equivalent color codes for various manufacturers.

Function	US Codes	Yanmar	Volvo
Ignition start	yell/red	white	red/yell
Ignition stop	black/yell	red/black	purple
Preheat		blue	orange
Negatives	blk or yell	black	black
Alternator light	orange	red/black	brown
Tachometer	gray	orange	green
Oil press gauge	light blue	yellow/blk	light blue
Oil warning light		yellow/wh	blue/wh
Water temp gauge	tan	white/blk	light brn
Water temp light		white/blue	brown/wh

Fig. 9-2 Basic Engine Starting Circuit

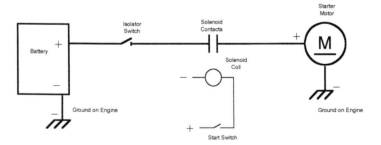

What are the basic starting system requirements?

The power supply to the engine starting system should have an isolator installed as close as possible to the battery in both the positive and negative conductor. The isolator should be accessible. Short circuit protection is not required. The isolator shall be rated for the maximum current of the starting circuit. The start cables should have an isolator as close as possible to the batteries, and accessible for isolation purposes. It should be rated for the maximum current starting circuit. The main starting circuit positive and negative conductors shall be rated so as not to exceed 5% voltage drop at full rated current. The main starter cables should have minimal voltage drop at full rated current. Cables should be kept as short as possible and as large as possible to minimize losses and maximize power availability.

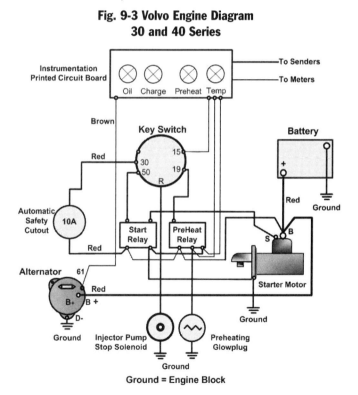

**Fig. 9-3 Volvo Engine Diagram
30 and 40 Series**

Fig. 9-4 Yanmar Engine Diagram

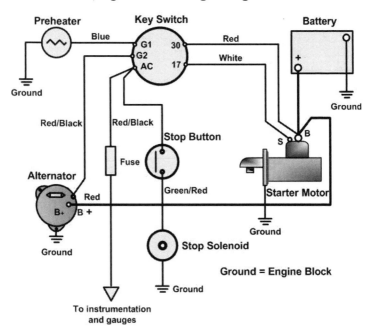

Fig. 9-5 Nanni Engine Diagram

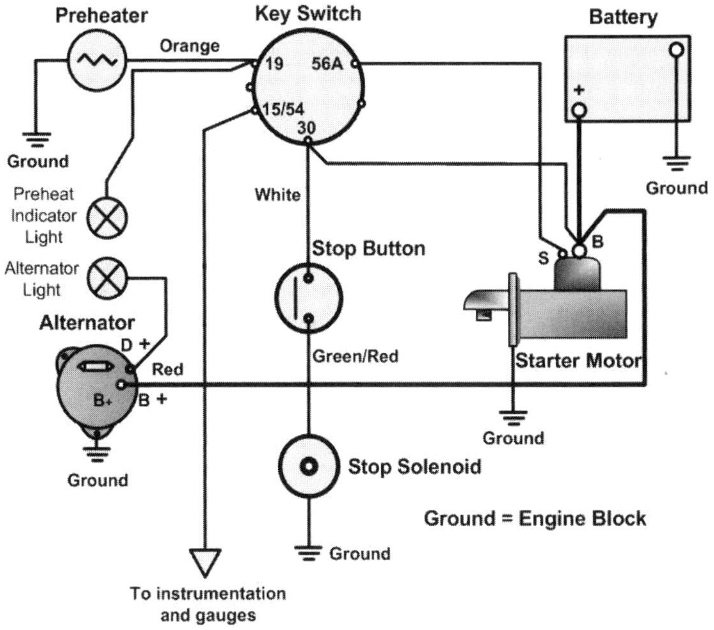

Preheater

Key Switch

Battery

Orange

19   56A

15/54
30

Ground

Preheat
Indicator
Light

Alternator
Light

Alternator

D +

Red

B +   B +

Ground

Ground

White

Stop Button

Green/Red

S   B

Starter Motor

Ground

Stop Solenoid

Ground = Engine Block

Ground

To instrumentation
and gauges

Engine electrical troubleshooting

Always check that the preheating system is operating, and the cranking speed is correct, as low battery voltages may not be turning the engine over fast enough. Check that solenoids are operating in the injection pump, and an audible click indicates this is operating. The most common fault in engine electrical systems is low battery voltage, or bad electrical connections.

The engine will not crank over

1. Battery is dead or very low

2. Control power has failed

3. Stop solenoid is jammed

4. Loose or corroded terminals

5. Start circuit relay is faulty

6. Control system fuse has blown

7. Shaft brake interlock switch is sticking

8. Neutral position interlock switch is sticking

9. Start button is faulty

10. Key switch is faulty

11. Starter solenoid connection has broken

12. Starter solenoid coil has failed

13. Main start connections are loose

14. Stop solenoid is seized

15. Stop button is jammed in

16. Starter is seized

Solenoid operates but starter will not turn

1. Starter brushes are jammed

2. Starter bearings are seized

3. Starter has mechanical failure

4. Starter windings have failed

Low cranking speed

1. Battery voltage is low

2. Battery terminals are loose

3. Starter motor is faulty

Engine will not stop

1. Stop solenoid connection is loose

2. Air heater connection is broken

3. Key switch is faulty

4. Stop solenoid is seized

5. Wiring harness connector fault

6. Control fuse failure

Battery is undercharging

1. Too many auxiliary loads

2. Engine is running at low idle speed

3. Connections are loose

4. Battery is defective

5. Alternator is faulty

6. Alternator V-belt is loose

Battery water consumption increase

1. The operating temperature is high

2. The regulator is faulty with high voltage

Battery will not charge

1. Loose or corroded connections.

2. Batteries are sulfated

3. Alternator V-belt is loose

4. Alternator or regulator is faulty

Engine starting system configurations

There are several engine starting configurations and arrangements.

Remote battery isolators

Many boats have simple mechanical isolation switches to isolate the engine starter motor power supply. In many cases, remote isolation have relay-type isolators. The control relay may be operated from a separate switch or interlocked to the main key switch, so that when the switch is turned the power is applied.

Two pole engine systems

In many engines which have dual pole isolated systems, two battery isolation relays are installed, one on positive and one on negative. The relay coil is connected to the alternator D+ terminal and this energizes the coil when the alternator is operating. In remote isolation relay systems, one relay can be used to energize both switches.

Parallel battery starting systems

Some vessels have a 12-volt power system and a 24-volt engine system. The batteries are configured through the relay so that the batteries connected in parallel are series connected to 24-volts when the engine start switch is operated.

Parallel connected starters

Larger engines use two starter motors, which reduces the motor size. The system uses a large capacity double-acting relay to supply current to both starter motors simultaneously.

What do neutral switches do?

A neutral switch is a switch installed within the mechanical remote control unit. It prevents the starting of the engine if the gearbox is engaged, as this could cause serious damage. A microswitch is used to activate a relay that is inserted in the starting control circuit.

Engine and transmission control systems

While traditional engine controls have centered on push-pull Morse control cables, there is an ever-increasing use of fully electronic systems. Manufacturers include ZP-Mathers, Teleflex Morse, Twin Disc and Kobelt. Systems may have an electronic throttle and shift arrangement or a mechanical shift with electronic throttle. Teleflex Morse have the TIS (Teleflex Intelligent System) MagicBus which uses the CAN (Control Area Network) protocol. In this system, all engine control and monitoring signals, data, transducer inputs and outputs share the same network. The following is a basic description of the ZP-Mathers MicroCommander system; other systems may vary but will have similar operating principles.

About the control head or station

The control head includes the throttle and gear change levers. The control head outputs a variable DC voltage to the actuators. Some systems may use a pulse width modulated (PWM) signal. The DC voltage value corresponds to the position of the control lever. The control heads also incorporate an LED visual and audible warning indication, and the control transfer button. The control head has three separate circuits and one common circuit. These are the potentiometer, transfer button, sound transducer and the LED indicator circuits.

What are actuators?

Actuators have an integral control circuit board, which accepts the variable DC command voltage, and converts these into mechanical outputs. The outputs may be solenoid valves and linear actuators, with drive motors and coils. These operate the clutch or transmission ahead or astern, and control the fuel rack for speed. The feedback loop to the control head or control modules is via gear-operated potentiometers. The control systems are essentially closed loop controllers. A set point is used; for example, the throttle is moved to the required position, the control system via the actuators increases engine speed to match. The engine speed feedback signal is compared to the set point, and when there is no differential, no further speed signals are sent to the actuators. Synchronization for actuators and processors is required in twin-engine installations.

How are systems wired up?

Wiring interconnects the control heads, actuators and any electronic control module (ECM). These include power supply cable, start interlock cables, and multi-core cables (in the Mathers system this has 8 conductors). The starter interlock cables are connected to the starter solenoid and the actuator, via a normally open relay. The multi-core cable connects the control head to the actuator.

Control modules

Some systems may have a separate control module. These modules include a power supply unit (PSU), and the microprocessor circuits (CPU) that input, process and output signals to the actuators. They perform the input signal conversion from the throttle and gear changes, and output signals to the actuators, via a distributed control network. Modules have displays to enable performance monitoring or troubleshooting using fault codes.

Safety and control systems

Most mechanical and electrical controls incorporate several safety systems and operating features. Redundancy is important within any propulsion control system. Manufacturers of control systems and engine management systems incorporate backup sensors if the primary ones fail. This can include speed and injection timing, throttle position, boost pressure for fuel air ratio control, coolant temperatures and lubricating oil pressures. An auxiliary throttle is used in Mathers control systems for a backup speed signal. Systems may have combination LED fault code and audible warning codes to indicate status and faults.

1. **Neutral Interlock.** A micro-switch activates a start-blocking relay, which prevents the starting of the engine when the engine transmission is engaged, ahead or astern until the clutch is disengaged. In addition, the control system has to be switched on and command acceptance carried out. Switches and relays can cause problems, so always look at this first if you cannot get the engine started.

2. **Shaft Brake Interlock and Control.** Shaft brakes incorporate a sensor that interlocks engine starting until the brake is off. Switches can cause problems and should be checked.

3. **Reduction Gear Oil Pressure Interlock.** If gear oil pressure fails to build up or falls, the engine speed is reduced to idle. It is important to ensure oil filters are clean and oil levels are correct to avoid this occurring at speed.

4. **Drive Train Reversal.** This is also called crash reversal. The control sequences the shift and speed functions. When an emergency reversal is requested it provides the shortest possible time without damage to the drive train or stalling the engine.

5. **Warm-up Mode.** This enables engine speed adjustment with engine in the neutral (neutral fast idle mode) position.

About engine synchronization

Engine synchronization is used to decrease vibration and noise and reduce fuel consumption. It is an automatic function. In most cases, a leading engine is nominated and the following or slave engine speed is adjusted to match it. Some units use engine tachometers while others use a proximity sensor on the shafts that increases synchronization accuracy.

What is the trolling or slow speed mode?

This is for speed control below normal idle speeds. A trolling valve comprises pressure reducing solenoid valves. The valves are operated by a servo via a control signal. When actuated, a solenoid valve opens allowing fluid to go to a pressure reduction valve. CAT trolling mode limits engine speed but allows full throttle engine speed for precise control.

Installation notes

Typical power consumption is 10 amps, and a stable power supply is required. This should not be taken from the engine starting batteries. It is also recommended that two power supplies be provided, via a changeover switch so that control is available if a loss of one battery bank occurs. In noisy electrical environments, a separate and isolated battery supply should be considered. Shielded, twisted pair data cables are used to prevent interference. The CPU should be isolated from any boat grounding system, in particular on steel or alloy boats. Shielding at actuators and control stations should not be grounded to prevent circulating ground currents. Grounding of the shield is at the CPU only. Excess cable length should not be coiled up, but cut to fit.

About engine synchronizers

While some complete engine control systems incorporate synchronization, systems for retrofitting are available. Typical of these is the AccuSync made by Sturdy Corporation which is designed for installation to inboards, outboards and stern-drives. In these systems the actuator is placed in the helm throttle control to engine control cables. Speed signals are picked up from the nominated lead and follow engines. When synchronization is required and activated, the system will match engine speeds whenever the throttles are within 15% of each other. Correct installation is essential and electrical connections must be tight, in particular the ground. Power consumption is low at just under 1 amp when in controlling mode.

About electronic control modules (ECM)

This is a computer holding the operating software designed for a specific engine. It performs all the monitoring and control functions. The ECM also supplies power to the electronics; processes sensor input information; outputs actuator signals; processes and outputs monitoring information; performs diagnostic routines; and acts as a governor to control engine speed. When the ECM receives a throttle speed signal, it controls fuel injection and maintains engine speed by comparing required speed with actual speed fed back from the speed sensors. Speed is controlled through injection timing and the quantity of fuel injected. CAT also has electric trim, which allows programming of increase or decrease of current duration to the solenoid to increase or decrease fuel delivery. This is based on the final injection test and compensates for the variability that exists between injectors, and ensures smoother and more even running. Each injector has a specific correction code based on tests.

About engine pressure sensors

The sensors are used for boost pressure, atmospheric pressure and oil pressure. These sensors have three wires and operate on + 5 VDC to provide a variable DC signal. The wires are voltage, ground (which is a zero reference,) and the signal voltage. Typical operating range is 0.5 to 4.45 volts. The system monitors for short and open circuit, and if signal voltage equals supply voltage, it is open circuited, and if zero it is short-circuited.

About engine temperature sensors

The sensors are used for coolant, fuel, air intake and oil temperature monitoring. These sensors have two wires, and are resistance devices. They are also monitored and will indicate zero if shorted, and high resistance if open circuited.

About engine speed

The speed-timing sensor consists of a permanent magnet and a coil. The teeth on the camshaft pass through the sensor magnetic field to generate a voltage. The time between voltage pulses is counted to calculate speed. Additional teeth are added to indicate TDC. These are a two-wire device that does not require a power supply. There are typically two sensors, one on the camshaft and one on the crankshaft. The camshaft unit is used for injector timing, and the crankshaft one for more accurate speed measurement. In two sensor systems one acts as a back-up. On older engines, a single sensor system failure causes the engine to shutdown. The sensors are critical to the primary speed and timing function of the ECM that governs engine operation.

About throttle position

This is normally the throttle lever. It sends the requested speed signal to the ECM. It outputs a pulse width modulated (PWM) signal to the ECM. It has a 3-wire input, consisting of the supply voltage of 8 volts, the ground reference, and the output signal. The PWM output is a constant frequency square wave, either full voltage or zero, on or off signal. The duty cycle is the % of On time. In idle mode this is 10-22% and in high idle it is 75-90%. The ECM monitors the duty cycle, and if less than 5% or greater than 95%, it indicates a fault.

How do electronic injectors work?

The injectors consist of several components that include the tappet; plunger; barrel; body; nozzle assembly (spring, check and tip); and cartridge valve (solenoid, armature, poppet valve, and poppet spring). In mechanical systems, push rods and cam lobes activate rocker arms and the injector plunger and barrel. In electronic systems the ECM energizes the solenoid, which magnetically attracts the armature and lifts the poppet valve to allow fuel pressure to build up. The check lifts and is then injected via the nozzle assembly into the cylinder. At the programmed end of injection the solenoid valve de-energizes and fuel flow ceases.

Installation of engine electrical systems

The reliability of systems depends on proper installation, location of equipment away from moisture and heat and a clean electrical power supply. Units must withstand higher machinery space temperatures, vibration, electric currents, RFI and electrostatic discharges. Actuators are normally bonded to maintain equipotential levels. Many cables from control units and engine management systems use multi-core cables; most are screened and screens must be terminated correctly. It is important to identify locations where cables may chafe, have tight bends, or where mechanical damage is possible. Relay junction boxes must be mounted in locations that minimize mechanical damage, vibration and heat exposure. Troubleshooting is carried out by service technicians using computer based test programs. It is common to blame injectors for engine conditions such as misfiring, low power and rough or erratic operation. In many cases, simple faults such as deteriorated solenoid connections, wiring faults or loose connectors are the cause. Check them first, clean and retighten them.

10. ENGINE INSTRUMENTATION SYSTEMS

Instrumentation is crucial to ensuring that engines operate correctly within the designed parameters. Instruments may consist of a bank of discrete analog meters, or an integrated system with digital and visual screen displays; most manufacturers have such systems. The latter is becoming more prevalent, and consists of trend analysis, alarm set-point management, alarm logging and other advanced features. Check all sender unit terminals and connections regularly along with a test of all alarm functions, preferably before you start a trip.

Fig. 10-1 Engine Instrumentation Systems

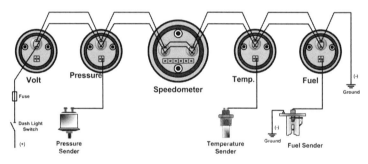

Temperature monitoring

The main temperature monitoring points utilizing the same sensor types include lubricating oil, transmission oil, coolants (seawater and freshwater), fuel temperature, after-cooler and turbocharger inlet air. The monitoring of pressures is fundamental to proper operation of any engine. This includes lubricating oil and filter differential pressures, fuel and filter differential pressures, coolants (both seawater and freshwater), turbocharger charging air pressure and air inlet pressures, gearbox and transmission oil pressures, and engine crankcase pressures.

How do oil pressure alarms work?

A pressure alarm either is incorporated into a gauge sender unit or it is a separate device. It consists of a pressure sensitive mechanism that activates a contact when the factory set pressure is reached. It is grounded to the engine block on one side. Activating it grounds the circuit, setting off the panel alarm. To test the alarm circuit, simply lift off the connection and touch it to the engine.

Fig. 10-2 Oil Pressure Monitoring

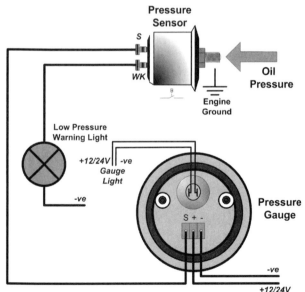

About water temperature alarms

These stand-alone alarm devices consist of a bimetallic element that closes when the factory-set temperature is reached. To test, simply remove the connection from sender terminal and touch on the engine block to activate alarm. The sensor has two terminals, "G" is used for the meter, and "W" is used for the alarm contact. In many boats, damage occurs because the alarm did not function or was not noticed. The first reaction is often "what's wrong with the alarm," not "what's wrong with the engine." It is good practice to add a very loud alarm, as some of the engine panel units are difficult to hear over ambient engine noise.

Oil pressure monitoring

The oil pressure sender unit is a variable resistance device that responds to pressure changes. It is very common to assume that the meter or alarm is wrong. Oil pressure sender units should be removed every year and any oil sludge cleaned out of the fitting as it can cause inaccuracy or no reading. Low oil pressure readings are caused by low lube oil level, or a clogged oil filter creating a lowering in oil pressure. A faulty oil pump can cause a lowering in pressure, a rise in oil temperature due to an increase in engine temperature, or an oil cooler can also cause a problem. When sender units are poorly grounded or Teflon tape is improperly applied to threads to make a high resistance contact a problem can occur.

Water and oil temperature gauges

The monitoring of water temperature is essential to safe operation of the engine. Temperature extremes can cause serious engine damage or failure. Sender units are resistive; resistance within the sender unit changes in a non-linear curve. If the gauge readings are not correct and a gauge test shows it to be good, check the sensor. Before you check the sender unit, you must assume that the main causes of high temperatures are: 1. the loss of freshwater-cooling caused by a faulty water pump impeller, loose rubber drive belt, low water levels, fouled coolers or increases in combustion temperatures. 2. Loss of salt water cooling caused by blocked intake or strainer, faulty water pump impeller, clogged cooler or aeration caused by a leak in the suction side of pump. 3. Increased engine loading caused by adverse tidal and current flows, or overloading. 4. Sender units are poorly grounded or Teflon tape is improperly applied to threads to make a high resistance contact.

Fig. 10-3 Water Temperature Monitoring

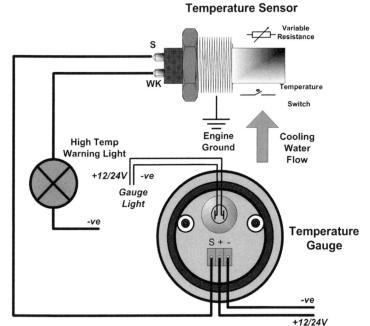

Exhaust gas temperature monitoring

Exhaust gas temperature monitoring is used in commercial ships and is recommended on all motorboats. Engine problems are easier and faster to identify than water temperature and oil pressure monitoring. These can be within the cooling water system; increased engine loads caused by adverse tidal and current flows; air intake obstructions caused by clogged air filters, or where installed, blocked air coolers; combustion chamber problems caused by defective injectors, valves, etc. Larger engine boats will also have cylinder monitoring, and this allows identification of problems specific to cylinders to be identified and monitored. Smaller engines will have a sensor installed on the main exhaust manifold. Pyrometer compensating leads and wiring should be routed clear of other cables to avoid induction and inaccurate readings.

Fig. 10-4 Exhaust Gas Temperature Monitoring

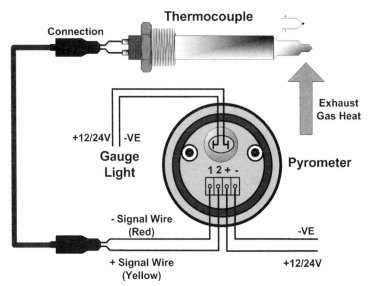

How does the monitoring work?

Exhaust temperature sensors are called thermocouples, or pyrometers. These sensors consist of two dissimilar metals (iron/constantine; copper/nickel; platinum/rhodium. nicrosil/ nisil, nickel/aluminum), which at the junction will generate a small voltage proportional to the heat applied to the sensor. The voltage is measured in millivolts (mV). The typical thermocouple consists of a sensing junction, and a reference junction. The open circuit voltage is measured with a high impedance voltmeter and is the temperature difference between the sensing junction and the reference junction. The thermocouple junction is also called the "hot junction." The compensating cables between the junction and the measurement meter are electrically matched to maintain accuracy. They are polarity sensitive and must be connected positive to positive.

About engine tachometers

The tachometer is used to monitor engine speed, differential or synchronization, shaft revolutions and turbocharger speed. This information enables decisions to be made on fuel consumption and vessel performance. There are several tachometer types, based on the type of sensing system.

The generator tachometer

This tachometer type takes a signal from a mechanically driven generator unit. The generator outputs an AC voltage proportional in amplitude to the speed and this is decoded by the tachometer. Variations in speed give a proportional change in output voltage and a change in meter reading. The most common fault on these units is drive shaft mechanism damage. Typically marked G and negative - .

The inductive tachometer

These tachometers have an inductive magnetic sensor. The sensor detects changes in magnetic flux as the teeth on a flywheel move past. This sends a series of on/off pulses to the meter where it is counted and displayed on the tachometer. Make sure that the sender unit is properly fastened. A common cause of failure is damage to the sensor head by striking the flywheel when adjusted too close. Typically marked W and G.

The alternator tachometer

This type of tachometer derives a pulse from the alternator AC winding, typically marked W. The alternator output signal frequency is directly proportional to engine speed. The pick-up is taken from the star point or one of the unrectified phases. Typical connections for VDO tachometers are illustrated. If the alternator is faulty, there is no reading. There are a number of different alternator terminal designations used by various manufacturers; the main ones are W, STA, AC, STY, and SINUS. If there is no output terminal, a connection will have to be made when you install this tachometer.

Synchronization tachometers

The synchronizer or differential tachometer is used to show precise speed difference between each engine in a twin-engine installation. Use of the meter allows balancing to be carried out.

Bilge and tank level monitoring

The monitoring of on-board fuel, water and bilge levels is an essential task. The majority of tank sensors in use operate by varying a resistance proportional to tank level. The two basic sensor types are:

The immersion pipe type

This sensor consists of a damping tube, with an internal float that moves up and down along two wires. These units are only suitable for fuel tanks. The big advantage with these sensor types is that they are well damped and fluctuating readings are virtually eliminated.

The lever type

The lever-type system consists of a sensor head located on the end of an adjustable leg. The sensor head comprises a variable resistance and float arm pivot. As the float and arm move relative to fluid levels, the resistance alters and the meter reading changes; typical resistance readings are in the range of 10-180 ohms. Lever-type units should be installed longitudinally, as an athwartships orientation can cause serious problems in a rolling vessel. In water units, the variable resistance sensor unit is located outside of the tank, while the fuel unit has a resistance sensor in the tank.

About capacitive sensors

This type of transducer operates on the principle that the value of a capacitor is dependent on the dielectric between plates. The sender unit measures the capacitance difference between air and the liquid. The sensing circuit outputs a voltage proportional to the level in the typical range of 0 to 5 volts. The most common fault in these systems is water damage to the circuit board, usually because of tank condensation.

About pressure sensors

These sensors are considerably more expensive, but very accurate and less prone to damage. The transducers are placed either at the bottom of the tank, or on a pipe to one side at the tank bottom. They are more common on computer-based integrated monitoring systems. The sensors output either a 4-20 milliamps or 0.6-2.6 volts proportional to the pressure of the fluid in the tank. The pressure value is proportional to the tank volume. If the sensor is located on a small pipe, it may become clogged.

How do air sensors work?

Air-operated bilge switches such as the Jabsco Hydro Air use an air column to pressure activate a remote mounted switch. They can switch 20 amps, and are ignition protected. One advantage is that they are less prone to jamming than float switches.

About charging voltmeters

Many instrument panels incorporate a voltmeter to indicate the state of the charging. As they have a coarse scale, they are only partially useful in assessing battery voltage states, but they are a useful indicator on the charging system. Many voltmeters have a colored scale to enable rapid recognition of condition: red for under- or overcharge and green for proper range.

Fig. 10-5 Voltmeter Connections

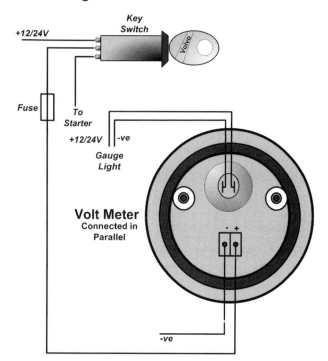

About charging ammeters

Charging ammeters are an easy guide to the level of charge current from the alternator. In most cases the level of current is not as important as seeing a reasonable level flowing. There are basically two types of ammeter, in-line or series ammeter and the shunt ammeter.

How does a series ammeter work?

This ammeter type is connected directly in series with the load. It has the main charge alternator output cable running through it. In many cases, the long run to a meter causes unacceptable charging system voltage drops and undercharging. An additional problem with installing such ammeters on switch panels is that the charge cables are invariably run with other cables and may be a cause of radio interference. If you are going to install this type of ammeter, make sure that the meter is mounted as close as possible to the alternator. If these ammeters start fluctuating at maximum alternator and rated outputs, this is generally due to voltage drops within the meter and cable. Also the under-rating of connectors is a major cause of problems.

Fig. 10-6 Series Ammeter

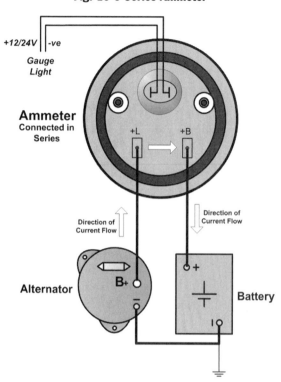

+12/24V | -ve
Gauge Light

Ammeter
Connected in Series

+L   +B

Direction of Current Flow

Direction of Current Flow

Alternator   B+   Battery

How does a shunt ammeter work?

The shunt ammeter overcomes the problem of long cable runs and voltage drops associated with a series ammeter. The shunt is essentially a resistance inserted in the line. Sense cables are connected across it and can be run to any meter location without voltage drop problems because the output is in millivolts. The ammeter must always be rated for the maximum alternator output. In many installations, it is not, and the shunt or meter is often damaged, with big voltage drops in the charging line.

Fig. 10-7 Shunt Ammeter

Shunt Closed   **Shunt Open**

Courtesy Blue Sea Systems

Shunt Ammeter

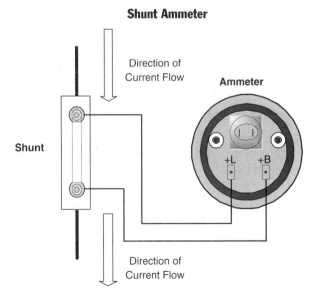

What about hour counters and clocks?

An hour counter is essential for keeping a record of maintenance intervals. Essentially it is a clock activated only when the engine is operating. There are a number of methods of activating hour counters:

1. **Ignition Switch.** This is the easiest and most practical method. The meter is simply connected across the ignition positive and a negative so that it operates when the engine is running.

2. **Oil Pressure Switch.** Although not common, some installations activate through the oil pressure switch, so operate only when the engine is running.

3. **Alternator.** In many installations the counter is activated from the alternator auxiliary terminal D+ or 61.

Fig. 10-8 Hour Meter and Clock Connections

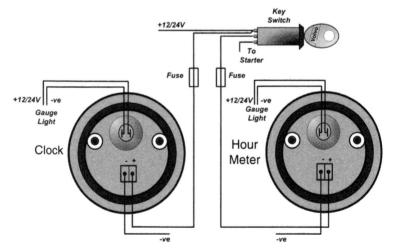

About acoustic alarm systems

Acoustic alarms are generally interconnected to warning light circuits, and the buzzer is activated by a relay. Acoustic warnings are activated along with a lamp from sensor contact W. The acoustic alarm should be activated through a relay, not through the sensor contact, which is not rated for such loads.

1. **Buzzer Test.** Using a lead, connect a positive supply to the buzzer positive terminal, and check that a negative one is also connected. If buzzer operates remove the bridges. Ideally, a test function should be inserted into the circuit so that alarm function can be verified.

2. **Operating Test.** With alarm lights on, put a bridge from negative to the buzzer negative, as sometimes a "lost" negative is the problem. Connect a positive supply to the relay positive, typically numbered 86. If the relay does not operate and the buzzer is working, then the relay is suspect. Verify this after removal, using the same procedure. Note that sometimes a relay may sound like it is operating but the contacts may be damaged and open circuited. If a buzzer is not operating along with the lights, either a cable or connection is faulty, or the operating relay is defective.

3. **Mute Function.** On many home-built engine panels, it is essential to silence the alarm. This entails placing a switch in line with the buzzer. The lamp will remain illuminated to indicate the alarm status.

4. **Time Delays.** During engine start up, a time delay is necessary to prevent alarm activation until oil pressure has reached normal operating level. Time delays are typically in the range of 15 to 30 seconds.

Combination system

The system functions as follows:

1. **Switching Relay.** On activating the ignition, the switching relay energizes. This illuminates the warning light and normally the oil pressure will activate the alarm.

2. **Time Delay Relay.** The time delay relay will be energized by the switching relay. The alarm contacts that activate the audible alarm do not operate for 15 to 30 seconds. If oil pressure has risen to normal within that period, the alarm will not activate.

Fuel monitoring

Fuel computers such as those from FloScan are typical of systems in use. Many factors influence fuel consumption rates including bottom fouling, vessel trim, propeller and engine condition, as well as adverse currents. Burning excess fuel is very expensive. Optimizing consumption by varying speed to the most economical for prevailing conditions, or altering trim tab position, are all possible based on accurate fuel consumption data. Performance drops show up in fuel consumption rates that can include propeller damage or bottom conditions. This can result in fuel consumption rate drops of up to 20% on a vessel with a clean bottom and matched propeller, and overall savings can exceed 30-35%. Flow monitors use a flow sensor, some use a paddle-wheel-based system; FloScan use an opti-electronic turbine sensor with an infrared light source to count turbine rotations. A processor calculates fuel flow based on the speed of fuel flow, and processing may use inputs from a log sensor or GPS to compute miles per gallon (mpg), liters per hour (lph) or gallons per hour (gph) rates. In systems with a return to the tank, a sensor is installed in forward and return lines, with return flow subtracted from forward flow rates. Engines such as Detroit and Caterpillar have fuel return flows at a much higher temperature than the forward flows, and compensation must be made for fuel expansion to eliminate errors.

Open sensor test

Remove the sensor lead marked "G" from the back of the gauge. Switch on meter supply voltage. The gauge needles should be in the following positions:

1. Temperature Gauge: left-hand, hard-over position.

2. Pressure Gauge: right-hand, hard-over position.

3. Tank Gauge: right-hand, hard-over position.

Sensor ground test

This test involves the bridging of sensor input terminal "G" to negative. The sensor lead must be removed and the meter supply on. The gauge needles should be:

1. Temperature Gauge: right-hand, hard-over position.

2. Pressure Gauge: right-hand, hard-over position.

3. Tank Gauge: left-hand, hard-over position.

How to test VDO sensors

Disconnect the cables, and using a multimeter, digital or analog, set the resistance (ohms) range to approximately 200 ohms. Place the positive (red) meter probe on the terminal marked "G" on sensor, if it has a dual alarm and sensor output, the alarm output is marked "W". Place the negative (black) meter probe on the sensor thread.

Temperature sensors

Readings should be as follows:

1. 40°C = 200 to 300 ohms.

2. 120°C = 20 to 40 ohms.

Pressure sensors

Readings should be as follows:

1. High Pressure (engine off) = 10 ohms.

2. Low Pressure (engine running) = 40psi:105 ohms, 60psi:152 ohms.

Fuel tank sensors

Reading should be as follows:

Tank empty = 10 ohms. Tank full =180 ohms

ACKNOWLEDGEMENTS

Thanks and appreciation go to the following companies for their assistance. Readers are encouraged to contact them for equipment advice and supply. Quality equipment is part of reliability!

Vetus	www.vetus.com
Volvo	www.penta.volvo.se
Yanmar	www.yanmar.com
Nanni Diesel	www.nannidiesel.com
ZF Marine (Mathers)	www.zfmarine.com
VDO Instruments	www.vdokienzle.com
Bosch	www.bosch.com
Parker Filtration (Racor)	www.parker.com
Dahl Filters	www.adiesel.com
FloScan	www.floscan.com

Log on to the author's website
www.fishingandboats.com

INDEX